Praise for *A Strategy for Daily Living*

"Ari Kiev's insights are invaluable. Reading *A Strategy for Daily Living* is time well spent."

—Bob Knight, Head Coach, Indiana University
Men's Basketball

"I have been a personal fan of Ari Kiev for over twenty years. Before the world ever heard of Deepak Chopra, there was Ari Kiev, offering his insightful, practical advice based on sound psychiatric principles. Each reader will draw from this book the kind of inner strength needed to cope with a complex world."

—William F. Baker, President,
Channel Thirteen, WNET

"This little volume packs a great deal of practical wisdom into every page. Dr. Kiev's insights into human nature, strategies for attaining success, and breadth of knowledge will benefit persons of all ages."

—Judah L. Ronch, Ph.D., President,
LifeSpan DevelopMental Systems

"With the update of *A Strategy for Daily Living*, Dr. Ari Kiev reasserts his position as one of the preeminent masters of American psychiatry. This book stands out in the world of self help as one of the best, and probably the most long-lived source of advice for patients. Far beyond that, it contains a wealth of knowledge useful for individuals in every walk of life.

—JAMES M. FERGUSON, M.D., President,
Pharmacology Reserach Corporation, and
Clinical Professor of Psychiatry,
University of Utah School of Medicine

A STRATEGY
FOR DAILY LIVING

The Classic Guide to Success and Fulfillment

Updated and Revised

ARI KIEV, M.D.

THE FREE PRESS

New York   London   Toronto   Sydney   Singapore

THE FREE PRESS
A Division of Simon & Schuster Inc.
1230 Avenue of the Americas
New York, NY 10020

THE FREE PRESS and colophon are trademarks
of Simon & Schuster Inc.

Designed by Carla Bolte

Manufactured in the United States of America

10 9 8 7 6 5 4 3 2 1

Library of Congress Cataloging-in-Publication Data

Kiev, Ari.
    A strategy for daily living : the classic guide to success and
fulfillment / Ari Kiev. — updated and rev.
        p.   cm.
  ISBN 0–684–83432–4
  1. Conduct of life.   I. Title.
BJ1581.2.K47   1996
158—dc20   96-42920
                                                                CIP

FOR JONATHAN AND MARSHALL KIEV

*The potential in you is new in nature and no one but you
can know what you can do, nor will you know until
you have tried.*

CONTENTS

PREFACE

Several years ago a young businessman visited my office with an unusual request. He was in New York City for only a day and was returning that evening to a small town upstate. He wanted a set of guidelines to follow that would let him function, without professional help, in the face of considerable confusion and despair caused by serious personal problems. "I want some kind of daily checklist to help me keep on track during times of doubt and indecision. I know I must solve my own problems, but if I had some general rules to follow it would make things a lot easier for me," he said.

Intrigued by this challenge I prepared a list of principles that were specifically designed to maximize his strengths so that he could cope by himself.

Several months later he phoned to thank me for my help and to tell me that daily he read through the checklist and that it had helped him to resolve many of his most pressing problems. In fact, he had begun to move in new and satisfying directions in his life that in the past he could only allow himself to dream about.

Skeptical of such dramatic benefits resulting from so simple a task as a daily reading of a set of guidelines (which differed from traditional approaches in not focusing on understanding and overcoming weaknesses or on developing willpower through repeated autosuggestion), I began to experiment by giving this daily checklist to various persons as their situations appeared to warrant it. Slowly, I expanded the guidelines into a series of daily strategies that were general enough to be applicable to a wide range of human problems and life situations, yet practical enough to help people cope with specific situations by relying on their own resources.

Eventually, I organized these strategies into a large mimeographed manuscript and a set of ten audiocassette messages. Many who have used them say that they were led to discover hidden talents and resources and that they have gained greater satisfaction from their lives as a result. At no time were these strategies intended as a substitute for professional help. Yet they have proved beneficial to people in a variety of emotional and situational crises. Indeed, I know of no one who has found them harmful, confusing or in conflict with any of their traditional values.

I have used these principles successfully for the past 25 years in my clinical practice and in my own life. The book has been read by well over 100,000 people. I myself have given it to over two thousand psychiatric patients as a supplement to therapy, as a general guidebook, and as a source of inspiration. Since it provides a comprehensive checklist of actions to take in the pursuit of specific goals, I have also found it useful in my intensive Life Strategy Workshops with Olympic athletes and others in helping them to maximize their potential. It is of special importance in emphasizing the value of a goal, the creation of a systematic daily plan of actions consistent with the goal, and a minimization of self-conscious worrying about reaching the result. It has helped participants learn to approach life and events in a proactive way with an emphasis on doing what is required without being misguided by inaccurate interpretations and automatic reactions based on long-standing habits, life principles, fears, and superstitions.

Increasingly, I have focused much attention on intuition, empathy and the capacity to experience the immediacy of life by encouraging people to live their creative visions and relinquish certain fixed habits of thought and behavior from the past. These principles, expanded upon in this book, provide a commonsense approach to daily living that emphasizes an experiential or existential approach to life. They foster a spiritual awakening by breaking down the normal boundaries between your "self" and experience so that you can encounter the immediacy of your life in a more powerful and meaningful way. This approach emphasizes the reduction of psychological defenses and negative self-concepts that keep you trapped in your intellect and in the repetition of the past.

As Shunryu Suzuki wrote in *Zen Mind, Beginners Mind:* "If your mind is empty, it is always ready for anything; it is open to everything. In the beginner's mind there are many possibilities; in the expert's mind there are few." This book highlights the need for a worthy purpose in life—not as a future goal to achieve, but as a lens through which to move beyond defensiveness, ego, and identity and tap into your human and spiritual potential for courage, love, compassion, reverence, and awe by focusing more powerfully in the present moment and choosing what you have.

These principles and practices will teach you to listen to yourself and others in a nonjudgmental and accepting way. When you do this, you will begin to tap the creative and spiritual potential at the core of your being. The principles of forgiveness, listening, active loving, and visualization will nurture your capacity for trust, love, and serenity and facilitate a level of consciousness beyond the "rational" mind where you can experience transcendence and transformation. This will enable you to move beyond the realm of memory and the recreation of the past to a new realm of beingness where your self can fuse with the world.

One of the best ways to use this book, after you have read it completely, is to review five pages and write down your thoughts in a notebook each morning before you start the day. This will help you to find your own answers to the questions and issues raised in the book and will slowly help you to formulate your own strategy for daily living. Each time you go through this cycle, you will tap deeper and deeper into your own creative and spiritual potential until you learn to live in the world with an incredible sense of serenity, at one with your true self and the universe.

Over the years I have known people from all walks of life who have found this book an inspiration, a life saver, and a wonderful catalyst for finding God and other miracles and gifts in their lives and in the lives of others. I have heard from countless people around the country who have found much solace and satisfaction in the book. It is my hope that you, the reader, will also find this small book to be of value in maximizing your efforts to realize your fondest hopes and aspirations.

ARI KIEV, M.D.

A WORTHY PURPOSE

At the outset, let me point out that this book does not contain a magical formula for leading your life. Nobody can decide that but you. Nor does it describe what you should do with your life. That, too, is up to you.

What I have set out to do is to describe a day-by-day strategy that will help make each day a more worthwhile one than the day before and will help you to tap into your creative and spiritual potential. A successful life does not result from chance, fate, or good fortune, but from a succession of successful days lived in pursuit of a worthy purpose. This book will help you to live, rather than merely await, such days.

I have written this book to help you set the objectives, goals, and styles of life that you want. I'll discuss how you can gain mastery of yourself and develop skills for dealing with obstacles that impede efforts to express your life vision. I'll consider how you can identify your strengths, what you can do to ride out upsetting emotions, how to circumvent obstacles, and how to control those habits that create conflict for you in relation to others. However, the guidelines I describe in this book must be adapted to your own circumstances.

In thirty-five years of psychiatric practice, I have repeatedly found that helping people to develop personal visions has proven to be the most effective way to help them cope with problems and maximize their satisfactions. With a vision, a person can overcome confusion and conflict over incompatible values, contradictory desires, and frustrated relationships with friends and relatives, all of which often result from the absence of rational life strategies.

A personal vision encompasses goals and objectives, but it is greater than a goal or objective. It is tied to an "ultimate intrinsic desire." It is tied to why you are alive, what you want to do with your life, what you were put on earth to do. The more you can define this or have a feeling for it, the more empowered you will be. As Shaw said: "This is the true joy in life, the being used for a purpose recognized by yourself as a mighty one; the being thoroughly worn out before you are thrown on the scrap heap; the being a force of Nature instead of a feverish, selfish little clod of ailments and grievances complaining that the world will not devote itself to making you happy." Vision is the stand you are willing to take and live your life by. It cannot be pursued for what it will get you.

Observing the lives of people who have mastered adversity, I have repeatedly noted that they have defined their visions, established their goals, and, irrespective of obstacles, committed themselves to their achievement. The moment they fixed an objective in their mind and decided to concentrate all their energies on that objective, they began to surmount the most difficult odds. If you acknowledge that your dreams and hopes are worth working for and focus your thoughts on achieving them, your chances of empowering your life will exponentially increase.

Reporting on the Scottish Himalayan expedition, W.H. Murray wrote: "Until one is committed, there is hesitancy, the chance to draw back, always ineffectiveness. Concerning all acts of initiative (and creation) there is one elementary truth . . . that the moment one definitely commits oneself, then providence moves too. All sorts of things occur to help one that would never otherwise have occurred. A whole stream of events issues from the decision, raising in one's favor all manner of unforeseen incidents and meetings and material assistance which no man could have dreamed would have come his way. I have learned a deep respect for one of Goethe's couplets: 'Whatever you can do or dream you can, begin it. Boldness has genius, power and magic in it.'"

A powerful dream creates a dynamic force for you. Consider for a moment some of the developments of our time—such as the manned flight to the moon—to recognize that dreams redefined as goals are the fundamental cause of all that has been accomplished by man since the beginning of time. Everything that has been created in the world existed in the thoughts and daydreams of some men before it was realized. This principle has been expressed in the aphorism, "What the mind of man can conceive and believe, it can achieve."

The establishment of a vision is the key to successful living. Edward G. Bulwer-Lyton put it this way: "The man who succeeds above his fellows is the one who early in life clearly discerns his object and towards that object he habitually directs his powers. Even genius itself is but fine observation strengthened by fixity of purpose. Every man who observes vigilantly and resolves steadfastly grows unconsciously into genius." Anyone who fixes on a purpose and pursues it can become successful.

Those who lead successful lives have made a disciplined effort to systematically pursue an objective rather than to drift about aimlessly with no objective. "The secret of success," as Disraeli noted," is constancy to purpose."

Most people describe their goals in terms of vague, indefinite conditions of life such as happiness, wealth, and fame. However, a vision is specific, with concrete images and goals that you, as a unique individual, wish to achieve or wish to have. If you can determine what you want you can determine how to achieve it, but even more important, how to live each day in the expression of your vision.

Why aren't more people successful? Because most people do not select and pursue a vision without regard for other objectives. Most people shift from one activity to another without any focused or directed purpose, naively assuming that things will take care of themselves or will be taken care of by others. George Bernard Shaw said, "The people who get on in this world are the people who get up and look for the circumstances they want, and if they can't find them, make them."

The most important step in realizing your vision is to define it. It only takes one outstanding idea to lead to your first fortune, to revolutionize the character of your life, or to change the nature of your work. If you have not yet decided on one thing you want more than anything else in the world, take some time to prepare a list of the things you do want. After writing them all down, choose the most important and record it separately on a single card. Put the master list aside to return to at a later time. The selection of a vision is, after all, not a one-time event.

Carry this card with you at all times. Think about your vision every day. Create concrete mental images of it. The more you keep it in the forefront of your mind, the more likely you will be to see opportunities and events around you through the lens of your vision and the more you will empower yourself to make your vision a living reality.

It's difficult to take charge of your life, decide on a vision, and determine how to reach it. If you are like most people, you divert your energy in many directions, leaving yourself with little energy, time, or motivation to pursue what you consider most important. If this is true, then you must understand the way you function now, how you can pursue your most important priorities first, and how to avoid distractions that keep you from this.

Many people complain about not knowing what

they want to do. It usually turns out that they spend much of their time doing what others want them to do. Because of convention, custom, family traditions, or other obligations, they have not learned to say no to requests for either favors they can ill afford to give or advice they are untrained to give. Nor have they learned to be selective in accepting invitations or commitments that divert energy from more personal interests and objectives.

If this sounds familiar, you need not feel apologetic in justifying your conscientiousness. Once you learn to be selective in saying yes and comfortable (and not guilty) in saying no, you will have time and energy to determine what you want. At first you may be uncomfortable with your newfound freedom and may revert to your habit of allowing others to take the responsibility for determining your life. Keep trying. It takes time and practice to develop new habits.

In doing this, try a mixture of self-discipline and imagination with regard to your time. Most people would agree that it makes sense to pay yourself first, to put some money in the bank before you start paying out your bills. You've got to conserve your own time the same way. Give time to your special areas of interest. When you have free time, you can give it to others in the ways in which you decide. People won't impose on you as much once you have learned to take care of your own needs first, since there will be times when you must say no. They will be reluctant to impose their requests once they discover that you're not a "doormat."

Once you have determined your vision, you can begin to create goals that are consistent with it. I am sure you have at least thirty minutes each day to list all your thoughts about possible goals. Try for ten ideas each day. In thirty days you'll have 300 ideas from which to select one or more objectives on which to set your mind.

It's important not to delay. Begin this exercise at once. While the thought is fresh in your mind, get a pencil and paper and write down five goals you wish to attain. Develop this habit of writing such thoughts down whenever you have them. Later on, add them to your list of possible goals. In the same way that a foundation must be laid before a building can be built or a course set before a ship can reach its destination, living your vision must begin with the first act. As Eleanor Roosevelt said, "You must do the thing you think you cannot do."

Remember, the more you believe that you will not succeed, the more likely you are to fail. Negative expectations result in failures, since they initiate the self-fulfilling prophecy. As long as you set up an expectation, you are likely to realize that expectation, to the extent that we become what we think about. As Frank Lloyd Wright wrote: "The thing always happens that you really believe in; and the belief in a thing makes it happen."

Take time out each day to plan your goals for the next day. What do you hope to accomplish? A succession of daily goals may suggest a long-range goal to you. Once actively engaged in your vision, you will find much to do and will develop an awareness of new capacities in yourself. Goal-directed activity should develop from positive assets. To the extent that you begin to define yourself by your actions in areas of your greatest strength, you will develop a new sense of yourself.

As Spinoza said, "To be what we are and to be-come what we are capable of becoming is the only end to life." The more involved you become in ac-tivity, the more satisfied and self-realized you will be. A vision will clarify your sense of identity. It will help you to pick the most important matters from a mass of information input and to strengthen your ability to say no to less important commitments.

However, living life in terms of your vision and working toward your goals must be done in the context of today's activities. Do not focus too heav-ily on the results of your efforts. Do not live for the future attainment of your goal. Live your life through the lens of your vision and what can be done in the present moment. Living your vision is not about reaching your goals. It is about living and working toward them. It is not about producing results but about living your life in a more mean-ingful and personally rewarding way. As Rabbi Tarphon, a second-century Mishna teacher, cited in the Pirkeh Avot (Ethics of the Fathers), "It is not incumbent upon thee to complete the work; but neither art thou free to desist from it."

It is also a good idea not to be afraid of failure. As Herodotus wrote, "It is better by noble boldness to run the risk of being subject to half of the evils we anticipate than to remain in cowardly listlessness for fear of what may happen."

Defining your vision and committing to it will help move you beyond the boundaries of your self-concept where you are trapped by results and a desire to get what you believe will fulfill you. The true source of fear and anxiety and the inability to be fully engaged in the present moment is living your life in a reactive way, trying to force it to conform to your concepts rather than allowing it to flow as a natural expression of your true nature.

When you focus too heavily on the attainment of your goals instead of on the process of living your vision, you will find yourself living too much in the future instead of in the present. As soon as you accomplish something or get what you want, you will become attached to it and then begin to pursue the objective, not as an expression of a larger vision of yourself and the world, but because you are caught up in wanting more of what you have achieved. An excessive dependency on the results of success will increase your sense of scarcity and insufficiency.

The same applies to looking for something in the future to complete you or fulfill you. When you do this, you cannot be fully engaged in the moment before you, and you begin to "split" or separate yourself from your experience. Writing in *The Myth of Freedom,* Chogyam Trungpa wrote: "Meditation is not a matter of trying to achieve ecstasy, spiritual bliss or tranquillity, nor is it attempting to become a better person. It is simply the creation of a space in which we are able to expose and undo our neurotic games, our self-deceptions, our hidden fears and hopes." The more we want to move toward our vision, the more we must accurately define our present reality.

YOUR HIDDEN POTENTIAL

Your life has been designed to work, and your hidden potential contains what you seek and all that you need in your life. It is OK to be who you are and to choose what you have. The Quakers call it the "still, small voice within," that place of full awareness within that is in touch with the entire universe and is the source of wisdom. In effect, you don't have to keep searching for confirmation by focusing on being someone else or being somewhere else. There is no place else to be and nothing else to get. You will be able to grasp the levers of change in your life when you can allow yourself to be present in the moment, accept the world as it is, and trust that everything is as it was intended to be. Thomas Merton put it succinctly:

"We have what we seek. It is there all the time, and if we give it time it will make itself known to us." Putting it another way, the Zen writer Senrin wrote: "If you do not get it from yourself, where will you go for it?"

Many people are dissatisfied even though they have what they believe everyone wants and should want—a nice home, a good job, and the like. They are unfulfilled by their achievements or acquisitions and even their relationships. But they don't know why they are uncomfortable or what it is they really want or how little effort they devote to what they really want to do.

What leads to this misplaced effort, to this lack of meaningful direction? Many difficulties result from faulty self-images learned in your earliest years. Much of your personality and your concept of yourself comes from the emphasis on some and the neglect of other features of your personality during your childhood. If this emphasis matched your temperament, talents, and special skills, you have developed an accurate and realistic self-image. If not, you have probably experienced much conflict. You may, for example, have an inclination to paint but were conditioned to reject it. The more you become aware of these suppressed sides of yourself, the more you will be able to accept and utilize your hidden potential. While your choices as a child may have been limited, they need no longer be limited. You decide what you do with your life. In the last analysis, your behavior, not chance or the concepts of others, determines your concept of yourself and whether or not you will reach the goals you set.

The requirements of society, which ask people to conform to certain norms, tend to submerge the uniqueness of individuals, especially in their early years. Early training creates many habits that may operate to excess when people are older—habits of depending on others, checking with others, and restraining one's self-assertiveness.

Unfortunately, the world that you were prepared for as a child is not the same as the world you live in as an adult. The limitations you impose upon yourself derive less from the nature of the world than from the poor fit of concepts you learned in childhood to your life as a responsible adult. To be true to your inner nature you've got to become free of these time bound distortions, which, though they may have made you feel comfortable, have at the same time limited you. As you correct your distorted perceptions of the world and accept responsibility for your life, you will see the world more realistically. Richard L. Evans said, "May we never let the things we can't have or don't have or shouldn't have spoil our enjoyment of the things we do have and can have. As we value our happiness, let us not forget it. One of the greatest lessons in life is learning to be happy without the things we cannot or should not have."

Parents impose their own limited concepts on their children, often ignoring their temperaments, special needs, and abilities. Your parents and teachers may have mistakenly ignored your strengths or may not have encouraged you to develop them. You can discover your basic capacities by experimenting with things that you always wanted to do. Don't be discouraged by notions that seem "silly" or "foolish" or "not you." Do it! Who knows what will happen? The Hebrew scholar Hillel must have been thinking this when he wrote, "If I am not for myself, who will be for me?; If I am for myself, what am I?; If not now, when?"

In some cultures, people can have two jobs. In others, this is unacceptable, and free time must be given to community or charity work, not to what interests you. If you are a woman, you may have been discouraged from engaging in business or pursuing a career. Pursuing such objectives, you may anticipate opposition. Don't expect encouragement from others, who may find it difficult to conceive of how you might be any way other than the way you are. If you follow your inclination to pursue your objectives, you will discover enormous potential for creativity and fulfillment within yourself and, in many instances, others—your husband or wife, parents, and friends—will respect you even more.

Focus on strengths, not on weaknesses. Focus on what you can do. Build your resources. Focus on the aspects of your daily life that you take for granted. You have more potential than you may think. Robert Fritz said, "If you limit your choices only to what seems possible or reasonable, you disconnect yourself from what you truly want, and all that is left is a compromise."

Consider how much your mental energies have accomplished for you until now. Your job, what you earn, your accomplishments to date have generally come from the application of your intelligence to various tasks around you. Like most people, you probably use only a portion of your mental powers. If all your accomplishments have resulted from using only a portion of your capabilities, consider how much you can accomplish if you tap your hidden potential. Setting up challenges for yourself by establishing goals will bring some of this potential to the surface.

Booker T. Washington said, "I have learned that success is to be measured not so much by the position that one has reached in life as by the obstacles that he has overcome while trying to succeed." For many, life has become too comfortable and easy and not challenging enough to spur them to positive action.

Tryon Edwards said, "There is nothing so elastic as the human mind; like imprisoned steam, the more it is pressed, the more it rises to resist the pressure. The more we are obliged to do, the more we are able to accomplish."

Encountering obstacles, you will increase the range of resources that you bring into play. What is it that you spend so much of your time on that diminishes the application of your intellect to the problems around you? For one thing, you probably spend a great deal of time worrying about things that have never happened or that can't be changed or solved personally, or you worry about the future and conjure up all kinds of fear about making mistakes or looking like a failure. You probably spend the least amount of time thinking about important matters or solving problems related to your objectives.

It is not necessary to search everywhere. You need only examine your present situation to discover unlimited resources and opportunities. But before you begin to give up what you have in favor of something that looks more desirable from a distance, examine what you do have, which is the true source of inspiration and satisfaction.

Ruskin put it this way: "The weakest among us has a gift, however seemingly trivial, which is peculiar to him and which worthily used will be a gift also to his race." The real trick is not in acquiring a greater fortune, more prestige, or more power but in finding out your gift and putting it to use. What's special about you? What is that unique combination of traits and attitudes and abilities you have that never before has appeared on the face of the earth? What can you comfortably do? What do you like to do? What do you do well? What do others think you do well? What do you do automatically? What kinds of things do you do naturally in your spare time? Stop and think. Are you using your intelligence and your energies to their greatest capacity? You probably use only a fraction of your abilities, and you probably don't use to maximum advantage other resources you already possess. Your books contain a wealth of ideas; your computer can link you to people and resources throughout the entire world, provide a vehicle for instant communication, and produce legible documents. Your radio and television are constant sources of information. Through the computer you can attend a university without leaving your room. One hundred years ago, the richest men in the world depended on many people to receive and transmit equivalent amounts of information. You may be ignoring what's at your fingertips. Think of it this way. If you sleep eight hours and work eight hours each day, you still have more than seventy hours of free time each week left to pursue your objectives. That equals 3,640 hours a year.

As Francis Bacon wrote, "A wise man will make more opportunities than he finds." You can prepare for situations that will occur for the very reason that you have prepared for them.

Edwin Huble Chapin put it this way: "The best men, not those who have waited for chances, but who have taken them; besieged the chance; conquered the chance; and made chance the servitor."

Opportunities abound around us, and it is up to the individual to take advantage of these opportunities. As Kipling wrote at the end of his famous poem "If," "If you can fill the unforgiving minute with sixty seconds worth of distance run, yours is the earth and everything that's in it."

Samuel Johnson put it differently: "To improve the golden moment of opportunity and catch the good that is within our reach, is the great art of life."

Montaigne said, "The great and glorious masterpiece of men is to live to the point. All other things—to reign [lord it over others], to hoard, to build—are at most but inconsiderable props and appendages." Your gift may be that which you do best and most readily. You should work to improve it. Others may discourage you from pursuing this, advising conformity instead. Don't allow yourself to be influenced. You need not feel guilty about doing those things at which you are successful, even though what others recommend may appear to be more important or acceptable. Following such advice may only lead you away from activity in the very areas of interest where you will maximize your sense of accomplishment and satisfaction. You must make an effort to rediscover the aspects of your basic nature that may have been submerged beneath the surface during your early years. At some point you have to take yourself as you are; you must recognize that you are equipped to contribute in some special way to the world, that you should not passively act in a way that is determined by others.

Perhaps your parents set you on the right track, encouraged you to study and to pursue a particular career. That's fine. But how you do it, when you do it, and whether you do it at all ought to be determined by you and no one else. Begin to reassess all that you do to meet the expectations and obligations set for you by others. Perhaps some of these things are not compatible with your temperament. Are you inclined to be meticulous and exacting, to want everything to add up to the third decimal point? Great—that's terrific if you are an accountant, a nuclear physicist, or a structural engineer, but I'm not so sure that the same traits will help in cleaning a house or selling radios and televisions. Each of us has inherited a different temperament. If you are an intuitive, artistic, and creative person, you'll be frustrated if you work in accounting. Similarly, if you like an ordered and structured world, you probably don't belong in a carnival-type atmosphere or in ambiguous situations. Different situations fit different temperaments. Familiarize yourself with your tendencies in order to size up a situation in advance, so that you can determine whether it is your "cup of tea." Avoid situations that upset you. If you feel compelled to drink at a cocktail party or in high-pressure social situations to feel comfortable, you are probably too anxious and would do better to avoid such situations.

Are you pursuing your dreams, or are you limited by beliefs and habits of the past that keep you from fully expressing your creative potential? Are you run by the need to appear a certain way or by the belief that you are a certain way? Have you resigned yourself to your fate and settled for feeling powerless and out of control?

If your answer is yes, then you may be paralyzed by your fears or stopped in the actualization of your dreams and not fully expressing your creative potential. The key to this is not so much learning how to reach your goals, but considering how you are stopped by your own thinking.

To liberate yourself, it is essential to learn to observe your thoughts and limiting concepts so as to see how you have created your problems, what you are getting from your problems, and what you have to do to get in touch with your real self. Shunryu Suzuki wrote: "Many sensations come, many thoughts or images arise, but they are just waves of your mind. Nothing comes from outside your mind. To realize pure mind in your delusion is practice. If you try to expel the delusion it will only persist the more. Just say, 'Oh, this is just delusion.' And do not be bothered by it."

Most efforts to solve problems intensify the problem. Efforts to eliminate anxiety create more anxiety. Efforts to control depression intensify distress. Efforts to do more of something or less of something or the opposite of what you are now doing to eliminate a problem only creates more of the problem. The habitual effort to choose something else, change things over, or find the "right" answer so as to solve problems or be "successful" or "correct" only traps you in your concepts and keeps you from spontaneously experiencing the actual events of your life. Along these lines, Shunryu Suzuki also wrote: "When you are practicing zazen, do not try to stop your thinking. Let it stop by itself. If something comes into your mind, let it come in, and let it go out. It will not stay long. When you try to stop your thinking, it means you are bothered by it. Do not be bothered by anything."

By allowing yourself to experience the events of your life without trying to analyze them, you can begin to live in the here and now. Then, you can begin to discover your hidden potential, your special talents and strengths.

You can determine those special talents or strengths in a number of ways, ranging from psychological tests to an analysis of the unexpressed wishes in your dreams. Remember, no one method works for everyone. You might start, for example, by clipping and pasting newspaper articles that interest you for the next thirty days. At the end of that time, see if there isn't some trend suggestive of a deep-seated interest or natural inclination. Keep alert each day to the slightest indications of special skills or talents, even when they seem silly or unimportant to you. Take note of the remarks of friends and relatives when they say that something is "typical of you." Perhaps as a child you had certain leanings that you never developed. Consider these as well.

From this exercise, you should be able to get some sense of potential strengths. Whenever you discover a strength or talent, think of five possible ways to develop it. Write these down on a 3 × 5-inch card and check them periodically to keep them fresh in your mind. You need go no further than where you are now standing to harness your strengths; and when you do, you will be amazed at how much inner satisfaction you will create for yourself. Remember, you have been building this basic strength all your life, although you may not have been utilizing it.

GOAL SELECTION

Living in the now is about living from your true self or center and choosing what you have. Looking elsewhere for the answer generally splits you psychologically and reinforces the erroneous notion that your problem is due to your circumstances or the people in your life. In fact, there may be no problem. The situation you are in merely requires more commitment and willingness to live with uncertainty. The challenge of each situation is to make things work by digging deeper into yourself to find the necessary resources.

When you choose what you have, you eliminate internal splitting and reduce the pain, struggle, and consumption of energy that comes from looking for something that you are not and ignoring the strength that you have. Choosing what you have means to work with what you have in line with your own inner vision of your life. This means giving up the notion that when you have gained something or achieved something you will be fulfilled. St. John of the Cross in "The Ascent of Mount Carmel" wrote: "That thou mayest have pleasure in everything, seek pleasure in nothing. That thou mayest know everything, seek to know nothing. That thou mayest possess all things, seek to possess nothing. That thou mayest be everything, seek to be nothing."

This means to commit yourself to your vision and then act consistently with it, and to stop living passively out of the programmed patterns of the past. From this you will discover that life can be lived with more aliveness and compassion when it is lived in terms of a consciously chosen vision than when it is lived it terms of old, automatic reactions and interpretations.

Effort expressed through the template of a meaningful goal facilitates the realization of human potential. If you accept the proposition that the situation you find yourself in now results from your concept of yourself, then you should be willing to test the proposition that your present situation will change in the direction that you want it to as you gain control over your thoughts and attitudes. As you concentrate on your vision and stop holding onto thoughts of failure, self-doubt, worry, and anxiety, you will begin to realize your vision in the here and now.

You control the direction of your life. Only your self-concept limits you from achieving your fullest capacity. Since changes in behavior generally precede changes in attitude, action directed toward your vision will increase your sense of purpose and belief in the possibility of success.

How can you develop a self-concept linked to your untapped potential? First, you can decide on the kind of life you would like to lead in ten or fifteen years. This will give you a standard for making decisions about current activities and will reduce the inclination to compare yourself unfavorably to others. Learn to ask, "How would I handle this situation were I the person I hope to become?" And then take action in line with your vision.

If an activity has no relationship to your vision, you may realize that you don't want to choose it. Would the person that you want to be take on those extra tasks, drive a particular automobile, engage in particular business practices? Defining your vision will minimize your indecision in making choices about matters unrelated to your goals.

Many people promise themselves that some day they are going to "let go" and do what they want to do. Unfortunately, the day never comes. Only when circumstances push them to a point where they "have nothing to lose" do they do what they have always wanted to do.

Without a vision, your thoughts may become worrisome; your confidence and morale may be undermined, and you may be led to the feared circumstances. Without a consciously chosen goal, you will be inclined to see the world though old perspectives and your own emotional reactivity to events. This will lead you to focus on your weaknesses and the possibilities of error and criticism. This, in turn, will foster indecision, procrastination, and inadequacy, and impede the development of your potential.

The goal-directed person assumes responsibility for what happens to him and does not attribute misfortune to the environment or the failure of others. He learns from experience by asking, "What else could I have done?" He realizes that he can change no one but himself.

To reach your objectives, you must rise above the motivation to satisfy only physical needs and desires. Large goals require greater commitment and the postponement of present gratification. The greater the task, the more you must assume responsibility for managing yourself.

Don't focus on past failures or exaggerated fears of future failures. This can distract you from the here and now. "I have never done this," "So and so won't like this," and "We usually don't do it this way" are rationalizations for the failure to act. Similarly, a crisis may provide justification for inaction when instead it could provide the chance to reassess and improve your strategies for living.

Action will give you a sense of identity, will reduce conflict and inhibition, and will increase your capacity to make your own choices. Pursuit of your objectives in your own way creates a sense of freedom. Look for the greatest opportunity for change in the areas that you take for granted. Handle simple choices first, difficult ones last. (The more you deal with simple decisions, the easier your life will become.) Choice is more difficult in interpersonal relationships, marriage, divorce, and job location. Before changing these radically, consider what you can do in the situation you are now in that would give you the most opportunity to express yourself. Then explore ways in which you can increase your effort in these areas.

How many goals should you have? One goal should be sufficient. A single goal will simplify your life, help you to define an identity, conserve energy, and reduce dependency on others. Too many goals, conflicting goals, or impossible goals produce conflict.

Uncertainty about your goal fosters a tendency to lean unnecessarily on others, as if they were experts. This may lead to uncertainty and ambivalence and discourage positive action. Neither the "experts," adversity, or public opinion should deter you from your vision.

Focus on one objective at a time. Like a servomechanism, the brain, set on a target, will call into play those dormant creative and spiritual potentialities that will bring you efforts to fruition. In line with the self-fulfilling prophecy, your actions will conform to your expectations, thereby tapping more of your true self and bringing about the event. If you believe that you will reach your objective, you will continue to work at a task until you have accomplished it and will not give up because of the uncertainty of the result.

How can you keep on target all the time? First, you can think through the steps you will take along the way to achieving your goal—practicing, so to speak, with your imagination. Since the mind can think of only one thing at a time, this practice planning will reinforce your involvement in your efforts. You can facilitate your day planning by listing on a small 3 × 5-inch card your vision and the three immediate steps you plan to take to reach it. Checking this card each day will enable you to visualize your objective and to review the relationship between what you have done each day and your objective. This can be a very valuable checklist, even if it doesn't seem to suit your temperament at first.

Always have the next goal in the back of your mind, since the most satisfaction comes from the process of pursuing a goal, not simply from achieving it. And, above all, don't be impatient about reaching your objectives. Harold V. Melchert put it this way: "Live your life each day as you would climb mountains. An occasional glance towards the summit puts the goal in mind. Many beautiful scenes can be observed from each new vantage point. Climb steadily, slowly, enjoy each passing moment; and the view from the summit will serve as a fitting climax to the journey."

Everyone wants to be rewarded for his efforts. But don't, as many do, delay in making the effort until you are assured of a reward. Have faith that your rewards will follow your efforts, in accordance with the law of cause and effect. If you try to obtain the rewards without making the effort to earn them, you will find frustration and failure and will be denied the satisfaction of a job well done. An excessive concern for rewards creates fear about making the effort and leads to failure.

Living in the now is made possible by your capacity to reframe or reorder your experiences by relinquishing your habitual way of perceiving the world and tapping into your own creative vision or purpose for your life. This requires what the Buddhists call "skillful means," focusing attention and energy on actions in the here and now that are consistent with your vision. To do this you must learn to speak your vision and then take action in line with your declaration. This will lead you to see things that were previously invisible, new connections, opportunities, and possibilities through the lens of your consciously chosen vision, which enlarges the meaning of living in the realm of creation.

STEP-BY-STEP PLANNING

Having chosen a vision or worthy purpose for your life, you can next define a strategy of fulfillment that will focus your attention on the action to take in the next moment without being distracted by concerns about the result. Such a day-by-day strategy transforms stress and breakdown, failure and error into the possibility of breakthrough and miracle by giving you a perspective for processing events so that you stay on the track of your vision. Your formulate the strategy in terms of your vision and not in terms of your need to be comfortable or to accommodate the resistance or reactivity of others.

An important aspect of such a strategy is to live by your word and be willing to acknowledge deviations from your commitment to a vision. Do not use energy to mask errors so as to appear competent and in control. The key is to recognize when you are compromising and faltering so that you can correct your actions and bring them in line with your vision. When you can distinguish between events and your emotional reactions to and interpretations of them, you can create new response patterns that are consistent with your vision rather than continue to make reflexive decisions in moments of reactivity that keep you locked in the repetition of old life principles and habits from the past. In this way you will discover that you are not at the mercy of external or internal events. Consciously you can create your world by taking responsibility for your life rather than passively allowing the past to repeat itself.

How much can you focus your attention on tasks related to your vision? How can you change certain routines that you automatically follow? What shifts in your thinking and routines can you make that will enable you to master the reality before you without being caught in self-protective ways of being in the world? Such inquiry enables you to distinguish between reality and defensive thoughts that distort reality. It also encourages you to stop thinking about yourself and start focusing on the tasks in front of you. Keeping score or measuring results relative to your objectives enables you to ask what more can be done to produce results consistent with your vision. From this angle, breakdowns and deviations from course become opportunities to focus on what is missing rather than acting as triggers for a cascade of emotional responses.

Surrender is another important component of a daily strategy and refers to a willingness to relinquish control over events and to "go with the flow" rather than try to correct for and manage every detail. It also means to step into the next moment without fearful expectations about results or concerns about your image. For example, you can learn to surrender your fear by speaking in public or sharing your dreams and innermost secrets with others without focusing on how you may look or act.

Mastery is another set of skills or perspectives that you can learn to apply in approaching your life more purposefully. The first step in engaging the reality of experience is to acknowledge the anxiety or distress of the experience so that you can get past it and discover the true nature of the event.

You also have the power to master your fears and thereby change your life when you are able to acknowledge that the "you" that you think you are is illusory. When you can surrender your "ego" and other preconceived notions about yourself and the world, you can redefine your life and begin to live it consciously in terms of whatever concept you wish to choose for yourself. Choosing what you have is to appreciate the present reality and then to work with it to realize your vision. It is not about getting away from the present or seeing your vision as an alternative to reality.

Having determined your vision, focus on what you can do each day and keep at it. Deal with the here and now. You need only concentrate on the efforts you make. The results will take care of themselves. Excessive preoccupation with the future may lead you to exaggerate difficulties and to try anxiously to bring about results in ways other than through the maximum utilization of your talents.

Remember these words of Seneca: "If we do not watch, we lose our opportunities; if we do not make haste, we are left behind; our best hours escape us, the worst are to come, the purest part of our life runs first and leaves only the dregs at the bottom, in that time which is good for nothing else, we dedicate to virtue and only propose to begin to live at an age that very few people arrive at."

To maximize the moment, you must prepare for it. To achieve your goals, you must prepare yourself so that you will actually create the opportunities you wish to find.

Remember that opportunities can't always be recognized. Iron ore in no way resembles iron or steel. Only if you prepare will you recognize opportunities.

How can you prepare? Take your job as a starting point. Are you knowledgeable in all phases of your work? Do you know the origins of your industry? What new developments will occur in your field in the next ten years? The more you learn about your field, the more capable you'll be in recognizing opportunities as they appear.

Rather than settling down in your work at some plateau, assuming that you are likely to continue to function at that particular job until pension time, begin to look for ways in which you can grow within your own setting, ways in which you can become more valuable in your job or in your community or at home.

Don't be afraid to take risks. These need not be skydiving or mountain climbing, but simply active efforts in simple daily activities that are so often avoided because of the demands of courtesy, social obligation, or the need to act according to the expectations that others have of you. Make a list of ten steps you would take if you were the person you would like to become. Take that course that you have been thinking about; invest in what you have been thinking about; try a new venture; try a new route to work; try taking a subway if you have been taking a bus; try taking a bus if you have been taking your car.

Delay leads to more delay. Inertia, not lack of information, fosters indecision. Postponement can become habitual and can lead to nonproductivity. It may mean accommodation and revision of programs and schedules, but you must recognize that when you postpone your involvement in something, you will probably never accomplish it and will be left with memories of past wishes rather than of past deeds.

Bypass obstacles by initiating alternative activities. This reduces conflict and frustration and permits you to continue the pursuit of your vision. Focusing on grievances intensifies their significance and magnifies fears and worries.

Must you be consistent? Must you stick to your original plans? No. As Emerson wrote, "A foolish consistency is the hobgoblin of little minds adored by little statesmen and philosophers and divines." Generally, most of us remember only this portion of Emerson's quote. The rest is equally helpful. "With consistency a great soul has simply nothing to do. He may as well concern himself with his shadow on the wall. Speak what you think now in hard words and tomorrow speak what tomorrow thinks in hard words again, though it contradict everything you said to-day.—'Ah, so you shall be sure to be misunderstood.' Is it so bad then to be misunderstood? Pythagoras was misunderstood, and Socrates, and Jesus, and Luther, and Copernicus, and Galileo, and Newton, and every pure and wise spirit that ever took flesh. To be great is to be misunderstood."

As you begin each day, you have the freedom to try new approaches. There is no reason to think that you even have to stay on the same job or live in the same house. The more you discover and master the freedom you have, the more you will determine your own destiny. This does not mean you should rush from one situation to another or escape responsibility by making drastic or extreme changes. Freedom is not license, nor should you become the servant or slave of your own impulses. You, not the situation, can and should change.

Stop and think what you can change in the smallest areas of your daily life. If you have been wearing black shoes, try brown ones. If you have been wearing striped ties, try dotted ones. If you have been wearing dull, conservative suits, try a sports jacket. Try a different hairstyle; try different routes. Such small changes will generate challenge and excitement, will demonstrate the impact you can have over your own destiny, and will spur you on toward fulfilling your objectives.

The modern world makes innumerable demands on an individual's time and resources. This creates conflicts and psychological stress. Despite limited time, you may overcommit yourself, leaving little time for your most important activities. Every activity that consumes time in the present must be assessed in terms of your priorities. To accomplish your objective, you must develop the habit of doing first things first.

Daily goals that can be achieved will help you to focus on the present. A simple guideline for accomplishing this would be to spend several minutes each night planning for the next day's activities and only those activities that you can actually engage in. Schedule your time in terms of these activities. The plan will enable you to get going right away the next day, and the time schedule will help you in conserving time for yourself. James Russell Lowell once said: "No man is born into the world whose work is not born with him. There is always work and tools to work with for those who will, and blessed are the horny hands of toil. The busy world shoves angrily aside the man whose hands are idle until occasion tells him what to do; and he who waits to have his task marked out shall die and leave his errand unfulfilled."

Focus on what you can do with what you have at hand. Do one thing at a time. Don't get flustered and confused by trying to do several things at once. Too many activities will inundate you and create a feeling of failure. Sit down and write out the three most important tasks you want to accomplish tomorrow. Focus all the effort you can on the essentials of each task. Start with the first, then move on to the next. It may be that at first you can only devote one hour a day to the activity that really matters to you. But even one hour a day can really add up. One hour a day will mean seven hours a week, 365 hours a year, and 3,650 hours in ten years. You can accomplish much in that period of time: taking a course, writing a book, painting a portrait. You certainly have one hour a day, even if you divide it into six ten-minute periods. What can you do with ten minutes? In ten minutes you can do some exercises and get your circulation moving again; you can write a letter to a friend, make three phone calls, get out some bills, or play a quick game of handball.

Measuring time spent in various activities will help you to determine how much you are focusing on your highest priorities. For one week, record the amount of time you spend chatting on the telephone. Also note with whom and about what you talk. This can illuminate how much time you spend profitably and how much you waste in idle conversation. You may be spending time with others against your better judgment because of feelings of obligation or as an excuse for not using your time to satisfy your own personal needs and desires.

You may feel that people are blocking you from doing what you want to do. Most people want to keep things the same. In this modern world, where everything is changing so rapidly, people make a conscious effort to sustain the familiar and continue with the past. As a result others may find it hard to adjust to your new direction, which may not fit their concept of you and may evoke anxiety. Don't be deterred by this. In fact, when people start questioning you about your new attitudes, take it as a clue that you have begun to move in the new direction you have set for yourself.

Stop and think. What has given you difficulty? Most likely, it is the failure to strive for a worthy objective and to become involved in activities compatible with your temperament and your talents. As a result, you have failed to gain the sense of self-realization that comes from the expression of these talents. Here, too, don't allow preconceived notions of what you can accomplish govern your behavior. Don't decide beforehand that you won't be able to accomplish something or that you won't be allowed to do it. Try and try again. Winston Churchill perhaps said it best: "Never give in. Never. Never. Never. Never." With persistence you can accomplish almost anything you set your mind to accomplish. Even Babe Ruth struck out 1,330 times. The man who hasn't made mistakes hasn't been involved in what he's been doing. Don't worry about errors. They are a source of information about what needs to be added or subtracted from your efforts.

To ensure success, divide your activity into stages and focus on the most important steps and on those most likely to produce first results by the end of the day. When you first begin a task, immediate results will reinforce your confidence and enable you to sustain even greater and longer periods of continued activity without results.

A common error is to shun activity to avoid error or to withdraw from complicated tasks before completing them. Redefine the activity. Divide it up into its component parts. Start doing what you can do now! You can modify your course of action more readily when you are in motion than when you are standing still. If you lack a sense of achievement from involvement in too many activities, reduce the number. Set objectives that can be achieved each day as well as over longer periods of time.

The more you break tasks down into their elementary components, particularly into those that you are in fact able to do, the more you will be able to accomplish the more difficult and complicated tasks. Above all, you must overcome the inclination to minimize the significance of the things you do readily, concentrating on those things that you have difficulty doing and that continue to reinforce your negative image of yourself. What you do well is certainly worthwhile. The more you can strengthen this, the more capable and satisfied you will become, thereby reducing the significance of your weaknesses. The belief that you can't do something is merely a rationalization for unwillingness to take a risk.

Proceed step by step. If you want, you can fly a jet plane. If you can't fly now, you can take lessons and build up training, experience, and flying hours, advancing from a Piper Cub to a Lear jet. You may, of course, encounter physical limitations or age requirements. Fine, but take it as far as you can. Don't say, "Well, that's not for me, even though I'd like to do it." If you'd like to do it, you can do it if you follow the necessary steps.

According to Ernest Newman, the English music critic, "The greatest composer does not sit down to work because he is inspired, but becomes inspired because he is working. Beethoven, Wagner, Bach, and Mozart settled down day after day to the job in hand with as much regularity as an accountant settles down each day to his figures. They didn't waste time waiting for inspiration." An overriding goal governed the activities of these composers and others, enabling them to overcome the most extreme handicaps. Activity itself generates the impetus for further activity.

MODIFICATION OF BEHAVIOR

Efforts to change your automatic responses, interpretations, and reactions to the events of your life will only keep you locked into vicious circles of the past and trapped by dominating life principles. If you try to be someone other than who you are, you will still be the same person you were before you started to "change" your life. The issue is not to "solve" your "problem" or "change" the elements of your life or "get something" you lacked earlier in life, but to surrender to your life by choosing what you have and living out of a new and more expanded vision of possibility. When you do this you will find that what you have is sufficient to provide you with all the opportunity you need to be fully present to your life.

Living by your word means to commit to a vision and then do what is necessary to realize the vision. In order for this to occur, you will need to learn new behaviors through modeling, or coaching, and learn to surrender by relaxing into your vision and riding through the waves of anxiety, uncertainty, and self-doubt that appear as you enter the realm of uncertainty.

By designing a strategy for the fulfillment of your vision, you will be able to distance yourself from the fears and automatic thoughts that hold you back. It also will free you from the compulsion to keep focusing on results. The strategy or structure of fulfillment is like a blueprint that determines what actions to take in the next moment and that relieves you of the necessity of focusing continually on what you must do to realize your vision. The results are the natural by-products of the strategies you have designed. To produce certain results you must design strategies of a magnitude and specificity consistent with the results. The strategy should help you to determine what is missing and what you need to put into place to realize your vision. When the results aren't produced you look to see what is missing in the strategy, not what is missing in yourself.

Don't put too much meaning or interpretation on the results. Failure to produce specific results only means that you were off target or were not in the flow. Ideally, the strategy will empower you to go beyond your self-protective habits of thought and behavior and put you in touch with the cutting edge of your life where creativity, courage, and compassion dwell.

Elbert Hubbard, a turn-of-the-century journalist, wrote in his newspaper *The Philistine* in March of 1990, "It is not book learning young men need, nor instruction about this and that, but a stiffening of the vertebrae which will cause them to be loyal to a trust, to act promptly, concentrate their energies, do a thing—'carry a message to Garcia.'" Commitment means to declare your vision and then do what is necessary and consistent with the vision to become the person whom you have decided to become.

LETTING GO OF THE PAST

When awake, thoughts are continually being generated by the very nature of brain activity. In crisis your brain will automatically respond to the diversity, multiplicity, frequency, and rapidity of new information that it has processed. How you will react will depend on how you have been trained to handle the information and how you have been programmed in the past. You can master a complex crisis if you can identify the important information, refrain from acting impulsively, and do not respond to the anxiety triggered by the crisis. If you cannot do this, you will be governed by your own untrained emotional impulses, which overwhelm your consciousness and impair your potential to respond intelligently.

You can train yourself to master the stress of crises. To do this, you must first recognize and then bypass all those thoughts grounded in superstition, myth, custom, and convention, which color your responses and attitudes and prevent you from assessing each crisis as a new situation with its own special features. You must train yourself to examine the facts, to assess reality, and to correct for the distortions you introduce by virtue of habit. A good example of this is the prejudice toward anything new or strange or unfamiliar. By adopting a scientific attitude, you open up opportunities for yourself to discover much that is good and beautiful in the world around you. By adopting, at the very least, a "wait and see" attitude to new situations and unanticipated events, you eliminate the chance of initiating a self-cycling pattern of anxiety and you increase the chance for your own personal growth.

How you think will influence the external characteristics of your life experience. What you adapt to will reflect what you want to adapt to. What you plan to achieve will be mirrored in what you do achieve, in accordance with the self-fulfilling prophesy that people tend to act to bring about that which they perceive to already exist.

When you repeat the past out of a need to survive or are attached to something in the future to complete you or to prove your existence, you cannot engage fully in the moment before you, and you begin to split or separate yourself from your experience. This is a major source of stress and creates anxiety and fear.

A dramatic demonstration of the limiting concepts of the past is the basic notion you have about yourself that you represent to the world. Your self-concept may be a social fiction that does not have the solidity and continuity that it appears to have. This concept serves to limit your capacity to function fully in the now, with total creative freedom in the next moment in terms of what is genuinely possible for you in your life. In fact, you are imprisoned by the denial of your impermanence and of the fact that you are not who you think you are. When you try to accumulate material possessions, fame, or fortune to define yourself and establish more evidence for your existence, you keep yourself from living your life in as fully realized a way as possible.

The stressfulness of a situation depends on your conception of it. If you view it as a challenge and act accordingly, you will master it and strengthen your capacity to master subsequent stresses. If you view it as disastrous, you will succumb to apathy and fatalism and will fail to take those extra steps within your power to master the situation. Once you discover that you can govern your own thinking and that in doing so you can overcome adversity, you will have gained the self-mastery that is inherent in all of us.

Careful preparation improves the capacity to endure hardship and stress. Individuals gain strength in direct proportion to their knowledge of the stresses and their familiarity with their own characteristic responses to stress. The more you understand how you reacted in the past, the better you can anticipate your reactions in the future. Knowing these reactions will help you to control them and to cope with the most severe stresses. This, of course, takes time; at first you catch yourself repeating old habits. Eventually you can anticipate and control them.

How successfully you behave throughout the duration of a crisis will always reflect how well you have developed habits of self-reliance and personal autonomy. To the extent that you can govern your thoughts, you can master all situations or circumstances in which you find yourself, since you have the capacity to grow and evolve toward the goals you select.

Few people receive real training in the conscious application of thought to problems or tasks. Only from efforts in this direction can you begin to realize the power within you. Rarely will you develop new strengths without some evidence that they always lay dormant within you. You should learn to search your past to discover these strengths.

You may soon discover that often you act not from an inner impulse, but from a desire to behave according to how others expect you to behave. Simple, everyday examples of this occur all the time—when you catch yourself smiling or agreeing with opinions that privately you detest, when you reluctantly share personal matters with others simply because they have pressed you for an answer, or when you willingly agree to some social activity simply because you have little to do and wish to avoid the discomfort of saying no.

When you find yourself behaving in these ways, you will realize how much the events of your day and of your life are governed by your own decisions and resulting behavior. A simple experiment will prove this to you. Try responding differently in one such everyday situation; observe how the simple decision to say no instead of yes or to refrain from agreeing with something you condemn significantly alters the ensuing experience. Once you have seen this, you will be convinced of the impact of your own decisions upon your experience and ultimately upon your environment. You may in fact be able to alter unfavorable circumstances by modifying your own thoughts, attitudes, and decisions.

Observing yourself will help you gain control over your thoughts and actions. In the last analysis, self-control provides the key to the mastery of stress. The more you attempt to observe your actions and the more you can recognize the influence of your own decisions on these actions, the greater will be your capacity to consider alternative courses of action in every situation you encounter.

You will not be pulled continually by the weight of custom, habit, or the social pressure to conform.

You can learn to apply this skill of self-observation wherever and whenever you wish. You can learn to concentrate and relax simultaneously so that, without tension or anxiety, you can concentrate your thoughts on the task or problem at hand and be confident that the outcome of your actions will be commensurate with your effort.

If you are like most people, you may be reluctant to direct your life in this way, to develop a life plan that will maximize your success or comfort. You may be reluctant to plan ahead in a situation or in a relationship—as if this were manipulative or dishonest and lacked spontaneity. Even though you know what you have done before, you may be reluctant to think through what you would prefer to do in the future—as if you must take as given what happens to you and must refrain from efforts to control your reactions and ultimately your own destiny.

Why is this so? Fear of change; fear of the reactions of others when you do the unexpected; fear that others will be shocked or hurt or angry if you act differently from what they expect of you. This guidebook has been designed to assist you to become more aware of such tendencies so that you can live each day of your life in a more rational way, capitalizing on your past experiences and your ability to assess the situations that you encounter.

The most effective way to deal with fear or anxiety is through the acquisition of information and through focusing activity. If you implement what you have learned, you will demonstrate to yourself and to others that you are not overwhelmed by fear. Study of a task and effort testing it lead to knowledge. Failure as a result of effort yields information that can be applied the next time. The same principle applies to criticism that, however unpleasant, can provide valuable information about ways to improve. Don't dwell on potential sources of difficulty beyond the limited amount of information available to you. Lack of information will only magnify your illusions of fear and anxiety.

To overcome fear of failure, analyze the steps you must take to accomplish a task. This analysis may clarify for you the skills you must acquire and may help you to devise a rational plan of action. Facts and skills will dispel fear. Every effort you make should be designed to provide you with more information, which will facilitate your efforts the next time. Rodin said, "Nothing is a waste of time if you use the experience wisely." Even unrewarding, unsatisfying, and unsatisfactory experiences can be profitable, especially if you examine what has happened. The more you know what you did previously, the better you will be able to prepare for future situations.

The human mind constructs models of future situations from personal experience as well as from information communicated by others. To the extent that your characteristic responses are built into your nervous system, you will respond to new stresses with characteristic responses. You can master these alarm responses and concentrate your intelligence on a practical mastery of the situation.

How you handle an anxiety-producing situation—on the job, in the home, or in the community—will depend on your own particular temperament, constitution, and way of handling things. You ought not resort to a mechanical formula applicable to others, but should use a method more compatible with your own particular way of life. People learn this lesson slowly. They tend to emulate others in their conduct of life rather than master ways suited to themselves. New situations require new solutions. The more you look for your own solutions, relying on your own assessments, the stronger you will become.

You can overcome fear and other negative emotions that inhibit positive action. While constitutional factors may influence your tendency toward fear reactions, you have learned your attitudes and responses to fear and can therefore modify them by knowledge and experience. Optimism and effort ensure the success of an activity. Don't find fault with others or with situations when things go badly for you. Stop and examine the extent to which you can modify your actions and revise your expectations about difficulties. As George McDonald said, "No man ever sank under the burden of the day. It's when tomorrow's burden is added to the burden of today that the road is more than a man can bear."

You may be discouraged; you may fail to accomplish your objectives; you may conflict with others or feel inadequate relative to them. Forget it. You don't need more ability, opportunity, resourcefulness, or other assets. But you may need to learn how to use what you have. Do you believe it's not worth the effort? Do you say, "What's the use, I'd better stick to my usual routine; I'd better do what my neighbors are doing. I'd better not stick my neck out?" If you do, you have not realized that the effort itself has force and momentum and will help you to overcome obstacles and create a reality out of what you may have only imagined.

Keep alert for situations that generate the five great enemies of peace: avarice, ambition, envy, anger, and pride. Petrarch said, "If those enemies were to be banished, we should infallibly enjoy perpetual peace."

Avarice comes from believing that you need certain things when you probably don't and from the feeling that what you depend on will be taken from you. Ambition arises from dissatisfaction with yourself and your activities. It's fine to set challenges and to want to succeed, but excessive ambition will lead you to set unattainable goals and to become too focused on the outcome. Pursue your objectives at a pace suited to your temperament. Concentrate on your efforts, not on the results. Citing the Caliph Ali, Emerson wrote, "Thy lot or portion of life is seeking after thee; therefore be at rest from seeking after it."

Envy comes from an irrational comparison between what others have achieved and what you have achieved. Lack of what others possess does not cause frustration, but failure to develop your assets does. Envy erodes confidence, fosters a "what's the use?" attitude, and reduces effort, when it should be seen as a clue to what you want to pursue.

Anger can envelop you and destroy your incentive. Whenever you become angry, review what has happened. Has somebody ignored or criticized you? Should that bother you? Must you depend on others' opinions? Have you allowed others to impose their expectations on you or control your behavior? What do you fear? And, finally, what purposeful actions can you take that will convert your anger into energy?

Pride develops from a need to impress yourself and others with qualities you lack. The mature individual acknowledges his limitations, acts humbly, and tolerates differences with others. The tyrant, depending on others to support a false view of himself, stifles his own growth and fails to realize the acceptability of his flaws. Your distress will vanish when you admit your fallibility.

"That which grows slowly endures," according to J.G. Hulland. Take your time; keep actively engaged in your tasks. Hardships, obstacles, and adversities may help you realize your vision. Misfortune strengthens. It teaches you what you can and cannot deal with and so prepares you for future adversity. As you master negative experiences, your confidence will grow.

The situation you find yourself in is no mere accident—it results from your habits and thoughts.

The seeds of future acts are planted long before each of us passes childhood. These early experiences govern our particular behavior. How you express these early attitudes depends on the experiences you encounter throughout growth, maturation, and life, and on the extent to which you develop a degree of self-mastery over your impulses and the inner dictates of your conscience.

It is curious that we become not what we want to become, but what we are. As life unfolds we are better able to actualize our true natures. Seeking a goal, you may encounter obstacles. Nevertheless, it is only through your efforts (limited by your self-concept) that you can achieve that which you were destined to achieve in the first place. Preparation for this goes on in the back of your mind, sustained by many quiet accomplishments that will gradually enable you to evolve toward what you can become.

How much you realize your potential is ultimately up to you alone, since only you can decide how much you will try to reach your vision. If you believe you can do something, you will never give up because of obstacles. If you believe you cannot do something, you will be more inclined to give up early.

If you focus your attention on environmental or situational stresses and seek to alter them, you will neglect the causative influences in your own thought and character that in fact determine what your environment will be. It may seem easier to change others, your job, or your circumstances. But unless you realize that you can change yourself—gaining control over the very causes of your life experience—you will not modify your environment one iota.

As you begin to focus on your strengths and not your weaknesses, as you begin to try to improve upon that which comes naturally, you will begin to modify your attitudes and actions toward others. They, in turn, will modify their attitudes toward you.

Your thoughts develop into habits, and your habits result in circumstances. To change the circumstances you are in, you need only change your thoughts. Your habits will change. Ultimately, your circumstances will change. If you seek to master stress, you need only examine the problem at hand, decide what you wish to accomplish, and apply yourself to the task of daily focusing your attention on the smallest increments of activity that will lead to the objective.

SURRENDERING TO YOUR LIFE

Choosing what is, or surrendering to your life as it is, means to accept what is and to let go of the notion that your life will be fulfilled in the future by someone or something else. It means surrendering to what you have rather than trying to change what you have. This is seemingly paradoxical but is in fact the one way to transform your life. Don't fight your feelings, accept them. Fighting them or trying to control them will only intensify them. Get familiar with your feelings of anxiety, panic, and depression, and they will gradually pass. It is better to acknowledge your feelings and give them space to be. Ride them out by accepting them as they are.

Surrender yourself to the immediacy of your life

by freely expressing your hidden and untapped potential. Surrender to the next moment without expectations about results or concerns about your image. You can flow with the events of your life by letting go of the repetitive thoughts from the past that separate you from your life and the world. Let go of the results and your concern about the opinions of others and concentrate on the tasks immediately before you. Learn to stand outside of the image, ego, or identity that is so intricately tied to the expectations of others.

The process of surrender is dramatically demonstrated whenever you go past the point of fear and step into the abyss or zone of real or perceived danger by doing something without certainty of outcome. Surrender can range from something as simple as standing up in a room of strangers in a workshop and singing a song to swimming with bottle-nosed dolphins in a marine port. Whenever you step beyond your habitual patterns of restraint and "rational" caution you enter the realm of uncertainty and open yourself up to the possibility of personal transformation.

I regularly demonstrate the process of surrender in my seminars by inviting people to speak to the group about their discomfort in speaking, to share their vulnerabilities or dreams, or to make a commitment to a future objective. These requests to speak the truth about their feelings or their deepest secrets often trigger feelings of panic in even the most competent of individuals. However simple the request, it is particularly dramatic when someone is reluctant to do it, which helps to demonstrate how fear of the reactions of others can keep you from simply being who you are.

These exercises demonstrate that the first step in activating your hidden potential and surrendering to the reality of experience is acknowledging your distress or whatever emotion you are experiencing that keeps you from being all that you can be. In the process of doing it, the fear and anxiety disappear, and you stand enlivened and vulnerable before the group and begin to draw on the supportive and nurturing power that comes from others when you are open and authentic.

The value of surrendering in the seminars or in

situations in life that afford you the opportunity of coming face to face with the cutting edge of your life is that you get to see that you may not be the person you think you are. The first step in becoming all that you can be is to speak your new concept of yourself. The self-conscious "you" that is concerned with the opinions of others is nothing more than the transient self-consciousness that soon passes as you stand before the group and share. When you are most "yourself" and fully engaged in the present moment you are least conscious of your "self."

The same holds true in other areas of your life when you are willing to take a stand for a new way of being in the world. You soon realize that you are more than your anxious thoughts and feelings and that you can in fact begin to function in the world in terms of whatever vision or purpose you are willing to declare. The more you share the fears that stand between you and your dreams, the more you demonstrate the power to consciously create the meaning, purpose, and direction of your life.

SELF-RELIANCE AND WEALTH

WEALTH IS, TO A CONSIDERABLE EXTENT, THE product of a state of mind. To live well and yet to be in constant debt, or to live above your means, will not give you the freedom of thought so necessary for maximizing your accomplishments. Many people earn much money at the price of their own individuality and sense of independence. It is not so much the size of your salary that is crucial, but rather the extent to which you feel comfortable about your standard of living, so that you can take the world on your own terms. To achieve this ability to determine your economic destiny requires that you reduce your standard of living to a level that gives you economic independence. From this point you can then determine ways of carving out new activities that derive from your greatest strengths.

Self-reliance and personal independence provide the most crucial ingredients for solving the problem of wealth. Personal independence leads to financial independence. The richest men in the world have invariably depended on themselves, not others, for earning their wealth. The more you recognize that you alone are responsible for your financial independence, the more you will find ways in which to earn more.

Is the purpose of wealth or accumulated capital to purchase new items at the start of every new fad? Or is it to help you achieve your deepest dreams? Is it to be spent on obsolescent devices or status symbols, or is it to enable you to implement your thoughts in active ways in the world at large so that you can further actualize your own resources? If you use your earnings to accomplish some worthy purpose, you will find much satisfaction and increased confidence in your efforts to earn more. The more your efforts to earn are linked to efforts to accomplish some broader objective, the more each will serve the other and increase your sense of self-realization. Moses Maimonides spoke about such choices when he said, "Since the power of doing good or evil is in our own hands, and since all the wicked deeds which we have committed have been committed with our full consciousness, it befits us to turn in penitence and to forsake our evil deeds; the power of doing so being still in our hands."

"He's lucky," you may say about the person who has accumulated a fortune or who earns more than you do. "I'm satisfied with what I earn," you may rationalize. And yet you may, as many do, feel you lack sufficient money to achieve your goals. Why should you accept any limitation on the amount of money you can earn in the richest country in the history of the world? Probably because you fail to understand certain principles about the acquisition of money. In his essay on wealth, Emerson said that "wealth is in applications of mind to nature; and the art of getting rich consists not in industry, much less in saving, but in better order, in timeliness, in being at the right spot." Efforts motivated solely by monetary reward invariably lead only to frustration. To earn money, you must search for ways to increase your contribution to society. You need only assess the nature of your skills, determine where they are most in demand, and bring your efforts to bear in the situation where they produce the most good. Money will automatically follow.

Perhaps you feel guilty about earning more money, even from your own efforts. Why should you feel guilty about working harder? Perhaps because you have set some kind of ceiling on the amount you are willing to earn. And yet, if the money was to be earned for a reasonable and worthwhile objective that would be a contribution to society at large, then certainly it would be of considerable value and well worth the hardships you might encounter. Many people set financial goals and then mistakenly remain content when they achieve these goals.

The acquisition of wealth results from planned actions designed to apply existing resources. Since money is earned from effort, not from luck or chance, you must focus on small, regular, detailed steps that can be readily controlled and that can lead to greater earnings.

Look for ways to increase your output in your present job. Establish financial goals: the amount of money you wish to earn, the amount you wish to save, and the amount you wish to have for your retirement. Record these figures on a small index card as a reminder of your financial goals. They may alert you to opportunities as they arise.

If you set financial goals far in excess of your present income, you are well advised to determine who earns that amount, how they earn it, and what steps you must take to earn an equivalent amount. Remember not to focus on the money *per se,* but on the activities that you can pursue to earn this money.

When you earn money, you will be able to measure the value of it in terms of the work accomplished. The dollar you earn will be valued by you to the extent that you have made an effort to obtain it. If you earn it lightly, you will view it lightly. If you sweat to earn it, you will value it more and thus spend it less rapidly.

As well, you must learn to spend money in order to appreciate its value in helping you to accomplish your ends. The value of money cannot be learned from hoarding it, but only by spending it in exchange for more desirable products or for items that will increase your capacity to earn more. Money is a form of energy; you must devote as much time learning how to spend it as you devote to learning how to earn it.

Money, therefore, can become a vehicle for enhancing your self-actualization. Unless you have this objective in mind, you are not using money wisely. You may use money to keep up with the Joneses. Certainly you should enjoy the degree of luxury that you need or desire. But self-actualization does not really derive from this kind of expenditure.

Money *per se* has no value. It is only a symbol of potential exchanges for things of value. And ultimately, it is symbolic of the individual's character. How you spend your money may reveal more about you than how much you earn. How you spend your money reveals what you value and appreciate in the world. Do you spend on others? Do you avoid spending for yourself because you feel you don't deserve the fruits of your labor? Do you trust others with your money? Are you in full command of it? Are you afraid to take risks?

A dollar in the hands of a child is not equivalent to a dollar in the hands of a gambler, an accountant, a banker, an investor, or a student.

More and more, money represents time and freedom and speed, for it enables you to conquer the globe in a way never available to the Caesars of old. It may mark the difference between the education of an individual or the freedom of a housewife. Tell me how you spend your money, who signs the checks, and I will tell you about your interests and values and the characteristic conflicts you are likely to encounter.

People often fail to recognize that money has no intellect. What happens to it depends on your values. Unless you know what you are doing with it, you may soon lose it. There is a great need to understand how you share it or use it to lord over others. If you learn the uses of money, you will learn more about yourself and about the opportunities available in the world. If you spend money in ways that increase your ability to contribute to society, your income will increase.

A practical key to economy is to spend your money, as well as time and effort, on whatever enhances your talents. As long as you do this, you will be building your strength and will spend wisely.

The acquisition of certain expenses that interfere with more important objectives can be vexatious to the spirit and can distract you from your true aims. As the expenditure of money increases, opportunities for diversionary activities increase. These may distract you from the efforts that first proved so personally rewarding.

Spend in relationship to your own self-realization and according to some kind of plan of action. As long as you maintain a balance of your expenses in relation to your income, you are in good shape. If you keep your expenses down, you can do what you want to do. The vision of a fancy estate for your old age, if it causes you to skimp now in the areas in which you have special talents, is a mistake of the greatest order. Spend now if you wish to maximize your achievement. To save all for a vague future may deter the fullest expression of your talents.

It is a society's need for certain services that determines the amount earned. Efforts in some activities may not result in the same monetary rewards as efforts in other activities. Do not begrudge others the money they have earned, which results not from luck but from the nature of their work and how they have accomplished it. It makes more sense to learn from what they do and then to decide whether one wishes to pursue a similar activity in a similar way.

Remember that you probably want more than you need, but that you are likely to settle for less than you could earn.

To summarize, spend for self-actualization and increased mastery, not just for pleasure. Invest your earnings in increments that add up to a whole greater than the sum of its parts; spend to increase income rather than expenses.

SELF-RELIANCE AND
DEPENDENCY

SELF-RELIANCE COMES FROM TWO SEPARATE ACTS: a positive orientation toward goals and a reduction of unnecessary and inhibiting dependency patterns.

Trying to meet the expectations of others in order to be accepted by them creates a compulsion to act in certain ways, which limits your own ability to fully express yourself. This is dependency. Talking at length about your plans and goals can diminish your motivation. Sharing your plans with others also creates pressure for you to meet their expectations and makes it more difficult to change your mind. Talking about your plans invites opinions that may inhibit you from taking action. Even when others respond positively to your plans, you still have reduced responsibility for your behavior. By making it a shared act, you have reduced the risk of criticism should you fail. However, you have also reduced the sense of satisfaction you would receive from succeeding.

It's foolish to ask someone who is in one business about your chances of success in another business. The chance of accomplishment has less to do with the state of the economy than with your willingness to work toward your objectives.

Avoid commitments beyond your means or capacity; these foster dependency, uncertainty, and perfectionism. Similarly, avoid the tendency to intentionally achieve less than you can, thereby avoiding the assumption of responsibility. There are numerous delays and difficulties in modern life that provide ready excuses for such avoidance. It is easy to blame transportation tie-ups and telephone-line breakdowns when you fail to keep your appointments. If you can't attend or participate or don't want to, say so outright. Don't make excuses.

Very likely you have characteristic ways of doing things, some of which produce problems for you. You can modify these faulty action patterns. You may be meticulous, cautious, and conservative, which may help you in some instances and may prevent you from acting in other instances. Often you must make choices or decisions without all the information available to you, even at the risk of error, rejection, reprisal, or criticism. Perfectionist trends present themselves as an excessive concentration on detail, procrastination, and indecision. Too many tasks may also prevent you from finding time to do what you want to do.

You may be so cautious and fearful of failure or criticism that you consider all alternatives before acting, attempting to avoid criticism by checking things out with others. You may never complete anything so that you won't be judged a failure. You can learn to observe your own behavior patterns to see how different ones trigger different responses in others. If you can identify these patterns, you have an opportunity to modify your own behavior, maximizing your control over yourself and the indirect influences you may have on others.

Suspiciousness also results from dependency and placing too much importance on what others think about you. Many people, at one time or another, become oversensitive to the nonverbal, and often unconscious, criticism, hostility, or rejection of others. If you find yourself reacting to real or imagined slights, don't argue with people over your impressions. It is unimportant if an occasional person has hostile or negative feelings toward you. Everyone can't like everyone else. Even if people are prejudiced against you because of your race, age, gender, or religion, that's their misfortune. As long as they don't do anything directly to harm you, you will be better off making a conscious effort to restrain yourself from trying to challenge them or influence them to change their attitudes. Accusing others of ambivalent feelings or lack of interest in you may frustrate you, foster conflict, and provoke the very response that you anticipate. Avoid any inclination to respond to sarcasm or innuendo. Acknowledge that everyone has a right to think for himself and close the discussion. Maintaining a positive attitude will, in the long run, draw positive responses from others.

You can change such patterns of dependent behavior through action and through the development of alternative patterns of behavior. You can't change the habit if you aren't in a situation that calls it into play. Developing alternative habits may not be sufficient. Often, the new habit becomes as much of a compulsive pattern as the old. You may search for advice, exercises, diets, or formulas, only to find that such solutions can come to dominate you and distract you from your objective.

You must deal not so much with the habit and the compulsion as with the factors in your present environment that reinforce the compulsive process. Focus on your attitudes toward other people. Are you too concerned about what they think of you? Are you afraid of criticism? Do you focus on goals beyond your capacity? Does your perfectionism mask an underlying depression? If these patterns sound familiar, you ought to take stock and define goals more compatible with your interests, needs, and skills. To do this, you may have to risk criticism and even the anger of others. But only by acting in this independent way, learning to say no to the demands of others and yourself, will you develop confidence.

Ask yourself, "What factors in my life are draining me? To what extent am I neglecting my own needs?" Are you known as someone with strong shoulders, willing to assume all kinds of burdens? Are you known as someone who is easy to approach, so that friends, relatives, and others feel no hesitancy about imposing on your time? Positive gratification from this must be weighed against the negative price you pay in giving up free choice. Don't worry about refusing requests that seem to be demanding of yourself. It is better over the long haul for families and friends to know that what you do for them you do willingly—because you want to, and not because you hadn't enough courage to say no or enough faith in them to believe that they would support you, whatever your reasons for not helping.

Assuming responsibility that rightfully belongs to others is not unselfish behavior. When you take over a job that someone else ought to do, you are either showing them that they are really unreliable and that you can do it better; or worse still, that you are kinder and more solicitous of them than they are of you. You have done what they should have done. No wonder you don't believe their expressions of gratitude and feel angry with yourself and those you have "helped."

Don't assume responsibility for the behavior or attitudes of others. Nor must you have all the answers. Don't try to control the feelings of your children or your spouse toward you by compromising yourself. Don't continually modify your own behavior so that others respond more favorably. Failure to recognize life's critical moments, frustrations, and failures causes this pampering of others.

It is not good for others, in any case, to have you assume the total responsibility for their behavior. A child, for example, learns as important a lesson when you say no as when you say yes. William

Boetcher said, "The man who is worthy of being a leader of men will never complain about the stupidity of his helpers, the ingratitude of mankind, or the inappreciation of the public. They are all a part of the great game of life. To meet them and overcome them and not to go down before them in disgust, discouragement, or defeat, that is the final proof of power."

Develop a recreational interest that absorbs your attention and efforts. Techniques of relaxation, passivity, withdrawal, prayer, and exercise reduce the unpleasant mental concepts associated with anxiety. They reduce tension, and they can renew vigor and enthusiasm. These techniques can help control self-defeating and impulsive reactions to anxiety, which may lead to excesses such as overeating, alcohol abuse, and drug abuse.

By letting go of your fixed beliefs, automatic reference points, and need for control and predictability, you will begin to perceive the world independently of your automatic filtering or belief system and expand your awareness and open yourself up to the power of God within you and the universe. When you give up your attempts to prove your identity, you will be able to enter into the next moment without regard for what you think or feel or what others think and feel. When you surrender your efforts to convince yourself and others that you are who you think you are, you will be able to let go of fearful thoughts and be able to live your life as an expression of a conscious and expanded vision of yourself.

By letting go of feelings that you have been withholding toward those whom you feel resentment, you will be able to let go of much bottled up pain, anger, and fear. When you surrender to the events of your life, independent of your emotional reactivity and interpretation, you learn that nothing is rejected as bad or accepted as good. Once you have mastered this process of active meditation you can go even further and learn certain principles of passive meditation where you can let go of focused attention on positive visual images and open yourself up to the spiritual power within you.

Surrendering to the now turns off the incessant mental activity that projects negative images onto events. This reduces misinterpretation, distractions, and anxiety about future events and guilt over past events and creates a sense of calm. Surrender leads to an expansion of consciousness and increased control over your autonomic nervous system, which enables you to stretch your performance in any activity beyond conventional limits. This leads to a state of "active passivity" whereby increased awareness, understanding, and tolerance allow you to control psychological processes.

Nowhere is this better demonstrated than in the sport of archery, where any tension created by trying to control anxiety will be reflected in the tension applied to the bow and arrow at the moment of release. The skilled archer, therefore, allows thoughts to pass through his mind without reacting to them so that they do not interfere with his functioning. The best shots occur when the arrow is released effortlessly so that tension does not deflect it at the moment of release. At the Olympic level, the archer, the bow, the arrow, and the target are fused, and the archer's mind is "empty" of thoughts that might interfere with the action. In this intense stage of surrendering to the process, the archer may feel at one with his equipment, as if it were an extension of his own neuromuscular system. He allows his fingers to unfold as he releases the bow rather than causing them to unfold. The more he allows events to unfold the less likely he will be to interfere with the smoothness of the release of the arrow. Since the correct actions have been mentally programmed during practice, they now need only be allowed to function.

To surrender is to learn to "shoot the arrow" without holding on. This means to do what you can in a given moment and to let go of the result, learning from what you have done and then moving on to the next moment. This means to stop trying to redo the past and to stop focusing on what went wrong or what might have happened "if only" something else had happened. Visualize the steps to take and put yourself in a positive frame of mind. Take another shot or swing at the ball. Between actions relax, exhale, clear your mind, and begin to focus on the next action to take in the next moment. You can learn to risk yourself by focusing on the next moment and listening without judgment or a perspective colored by concern for the past or preoccupation with future results.

When you let go of the limiting reactions and interpretations based on old life principles and begin to be in the world from a new perspective, you will create miracles and breakthroughs. Breakthroughs occur when you see things that you couldn't see before and discover things that you never knew existed. They are characterized by being able to experience the here and now in a transparent way so that you are at one with your experience with a minimum of associated self-consciousness.

Breakthroughs refer to those moments when you are able to live your life as an expression of your vision rather than self-protectively in terms of your identity. To do this you must learn to live without certainty and without holding back to "conserve" your energy. Breakthroughs result from living experientially in the here and now through the distinction of vision. While this means living with uncertainty it also taps into your hidden potential and creates miracles.

Breakthroughs occur when you empty yourself of your preconceptions and allow yourself to be in the world in a different way, to go beyond constraint or habit in the face of anxiety, fear, or self-doubt to do that which wouldn't have occurred otherwise. Breakthroughs result from telling the truth without softening your answer to avoid hurting someone's feelings.

The ability to withdraw into solitude will also increase your faith in your capacity to achieve your objectives. It will give you strength to endure frustrations and uncertainty. Time spent alone thinking about your vision and the steps you are taking to reach it will give a larger purpose or meaning to your efforts and will revitalize confidence, particularly when you are plagued by persistent distressing thoughts of your problems. Woodrow Wilson said we grow great by dreams. "All men are dreamers. They see things in the soft haze of a spring day or in the red fire of a long winter's evening. Some of us let these great dreams die, but others nourish and protect them, nurse them through bad days 'til they bring them to the sunshine and light' which comes always to those who sincerely hope that their dreams will come true."

Unfortunately, spending time alone with one's own thoughts creates anxiety for many people and accounts for much escapist activity. Learn to listen to your own thoughts. This will help you to learn more about your inner self and your real goals. Spend some time alone each day familiarizing yourself with your thoughts. You can do this while walking outdoors or relaxing at home, in a church, synagogue, or mosque, or even in the public library. This solitude will provide you with an opportunity to clarify and become comfortable with your feelings and thoughts and to assess the strategies for reaching your objectives.

The ability to withdraw into such solitude in the presence of others will also prove an invaluable skill in various crisis and conflict situations. At times of stress or pressure, withdraw into a quiet corner to examine your thoughts. Don't feel obligated to act immediately. This ability to contemplate and evaluate situations in terms of your broader objectives will give you the strength and sustenance to cope with problems far greater than those you usually must handle.

Learn to "keep cool." Delaying your responses to others will reduce the urgency that magnifies the significance of events. Suspend judgment until you can assess a situation calmly in the light of your limitations and strengths. Delay will enable you to stand outside of tense situations, to assess priorities, and to decrease your vulnerability. To the extent that you control your life, your involvement in relationships and activities, when they occur, will be genuine and free of fear. Delay does not mean postponement. It simply means control over snap judgments. Make decisions when you are away from a situation and can think alone. In time, you may be able to do this in the presence of others.

RELATIONSHIPS WITH OTHERS

THERE IS A DIRECT LINK BETWEEN SERVICE TO others and rewards in life. Whatever you put effort into will result in reward. You need not give much consideration to the nature of these rewards or to whether or not you will obtain them, for they will appear to the extent that you concentrate on making the most of your efforts. Nowhere will this be more apparent than in your relationships with people.

Along these lines Confucius wrote, "He who wishes to secure the good of others, has already secured his own." This means that the benefits you derive from the world will be in direct proportion to the benefits that you provide to others. This relates both to individuals and to the public good.

Whom can you serve? Where can you make a contribution? Look at the people around you, your family, friends, co-workers, customers, and others whom you meet in daily life. To the degree that you provide or contribute to the welfare of all these people, you will be rewarded.

We live at a time in history when the world is fast becoming a global village. Nations are dependent on other nations. Communities relate with other communities. No one can be an island unto himself. It is impossible to live in any community without in some way providing some kind of service to some groups of people, just as it's impossible to live in a community without receiving the services of other people. The more you recognize this interdependence, the more you will want to make an active effort to cooperate with others.

Relationships are strongest when they develop in pursuit of a shared objective or activity. Relationships that focus simply on "having a relationship" will prove taxing, frustrating, and generally much less rewarding. Where differences exist in attitude, values, and objectives, do not try to modify the other person to suit your needs. Similarly, don't allow yourself to be so accommodating that you compromise your own identity. Find shared interests and activities and pursue these. Accentuate the positive features of a relationship; conflict and recrimination will subside.

Don't dominate or tyrannize others. The more you can define your particular skill and interest area, the more you can differentiate what you can contribute to a particular situation and what others can contribute. Not all activities involve cooperative effort. Many complex processes can be divided into discrete activities that one person can do alone. The contribution of autonomous individuals working together on those individual tasks that they do best alone makes for the strength that comes from cooperative effort.

John Galsworthy said: "The essential characteristics of the gentleman were the ability to put himself in the place of others, the horror of forcing others into positions from which he himself would recoil, and the power to do what he feels to be right without considering what others may say or think."

Imposing obligations on others to do certain things demonstrates fear, not strength. Strength comes from the ability to do what you want to do yourself. Examine all those situations in which you are telling others what to do without regard for their capacity to determine their own direction. Stop and listen to others. Recognize that they, too, have specific individual needs. You can help them if you allow them to pursue their own directions, not if you impose fixed expectations that you think are best. Listening to others will help you to understand what they want and how you can cooperate with them to improve your relationship.

Remember what William James wrote: "The first thing to learn in intercourse with others is non-interference with their own particular ways of being happy, provided that those ways are not assumed to interfere by violence with ours." Accept others as they are. Don't expect that they are going to modify themselves to meet your expectations.

"A man who desires to help others by counsel or deed will refrain from dwelling on men's faults, and will speak but sparingly of human weaknesses.

But he will speak at large of man's virtue and power, and the means of perfecting the same, that thus men may endeavor joyously to live, so far as in them lies, after the commandment of reason," said Spinoza.

When you have difficulties with others, search for alternative ways of relating. Consider this even if the other person is overly emotional, hostile, or vindictive. Examine how you detoured from your original course. Have you been discouraged by unrealistic envy of the assets or achievements of others? Continual comparison between yourself with others will invariably distract your attention from your objectives; rarely, if ever, will it produce any positive benefits, no matter how much you may rationalize the value of measuring yourself against others.

Remember what Emerson wrote: "There is a time in every man's education when he arrives at the conviction that envy is ignorance; that imitation is suicide; that he must take himself for better or for worse as his portion; that though the wide universe is full of good, no kernel of nourishing corn can come to him but through his toil bestowed on that part of ground which is given to him to till. The power which resides in him is new in nature, and none but he knows what that is which he can do, nor does he know until he has tried. Not for nothing one face, one character, one fact, makes much impression on him and another none."

Have you been sidetracked from your objectives by a competitive drive or social pressure to compete? This can dilute your efforts from activities in areas of strength, interest, and resources that will ensure success. Competition for prestige in areas where you lack competence may also create a sense of inadequacy.

It is amazing what a change in attitude can do for improving a relationship. You can prove this to yourself in the following way. For one week, make a conscious effort to find one area of mutual interest with everyone you meet for the first time. For one week, make a conscious attempt to listen to the whole story of those who seek your advice. Do nothing more. Don't give your advice, opinions, directions, or criticism. Allow yourself one week to think over what you yourself can do that will help others to help themselves. What is there that you can praise about their performance or attitude? What broader perspective can you suggest to them that will add an element of hope to their misfortune or excitement to what now bores them? What suggestions can you offer that will enable them to maximize their own resources in order to accomplish their objectives?

As simple as this sounds, you will no doubt find it hard to do, for it is hard to resist the temptation to sound like an expert or to delay response when others urgently demand solutions. It is hard to keep quiet when you believe you have the answers to someone else's problem.

What, then, is to be gained by this week of delay? If in the week's delay you consider the special and unique qualities of others, you will come to realize that the solution to their problems can really only come from their particular strengths and their style in approaching problems. Your own experiences in the same situation are less likely to prove applicable to them than their own previous experiences in dealing with similar situations. Ultimately, they can only do it their way; the best you can do is to recognize that fact and perhaps help them to see it as well.

If you wish others to respect you, you must show respect for them. For twenty days, approach everyone you meet, irrespective of station in life, as if he were the most important person in the world. Everyone wants to feel that he counts for something and is important to someone. Invariably, people will give their love, respect, and attention to the person who fills that need. Consideration for others generally reflects faith in self and faith in others.

For the next twenty days, act toward others as you would want them to act toward you. Treat others as they want to be treated. Approach each day as if you were the most successful person in the whole world. This attitude will readily become a major bulwark against petty irritations and misfortune. Faith in yourself and in others will help you to keep your head when you encounter daredevils on the highway or when problems are dumped on your desk. Faith in yourself and in the world around you will enable you to overlook the foibles of mankind; you will pursue your course rather than slip into an attitude of frustration and anger.

Remember that association with others does not mean that you have to define yourself in terms of membership in a clique or group. Prejudice derives from people's eagerness to be accepted by a group of like-minded people who provide mutual support by excluding others. The creation of an "out-group" automatically defines the "in-group." Become your own in-group. As Washington Irving wrote, "There is a healthful heartiness about real dignity that never dreads contact and communion with others, however humble."

How often have you refused to associate with someone because you found him stupid or ignorant or because you didn't agree with him? How often have you ridiculed, criticized, or scorned others because they were of a lower station or had less education than you? Don't be afraid to associate with people whom your neighbors may consider "ne'er do wells" or "foreigners." How many of your friends are just like you—of the same school, with the same education, of the same religion, the same economic group, and so forth? I'm not sure you can learn very much that way. You can learn much more by recognizing that there is something to be learned from everybody. Each of us has a story to tell and a unique perspective on the world. The way to understand the world is to see it from as many viewpoints as possible.

You don't have to accept other views, but openness to ideas will help in the discovery of your own viewpoint. As you clarify your own views, your interest in the perceptions of others will increase. Recognize the limitations of your own perspective. Others have their own truths, which are just as valid for them. Theodore Roosevelt said: "There is a point, of course, where a man must take the isolated peak and break with all his associates for clear principle; but until that time comes he must work, if he would be of use, with men as they are. As long as the good in them over-balances the evil, let him work with them for the best that can be obtained."

Until you can leave a group without fear of being rejected, you will be under pressure to conform.

How can you reduce this pressure? Focus on your goals, reduce communication overload, avoid preoccupation with the past and future, avoid envy of the activities or achievements of others, and avoid competition. Possessiveness, jealousy, unreasonable demands, and neurotic obligations to conform to the expectations of others must also be avoided.

The practice of forgiveness can play an important role in your relationships with others. Forgiveness will enable you to correct distortions in your relationships and to improve the quality, intensity, and meaningfulness of relationships. It means letting go of past resentments toward others so that you can experience them in the present. Even if you do not "feel" like forgiving someone, forgiving them will release you from the hold of the past and allow you to experience the world in a new way. To forgive is to step outside the vicious circle of interpretation, where concepts from the past dominate experience, and to begin to live in terms of a larger more worthy purpose.

Forgiveness eliminates fear and anxiety, weakness and vulnerability. It loosens the hold of past memories and experiences that keep you locked into a predictable repetition of the past and prevent you from experiencing the present. Forgiveness, as a vision of the future, frees you from the rigid and inflexible posture you maintain toward others and allows you to see them in a new light.

Forgiveness means letting go of the belief that your happiness and peace of mind depend on others or on factors outside yourself and recognizing that the answer ultimately resides within. If you can drop your social-self or ego defense systems and declare forgiveness as a new way of being in the world, you will get in touch with your spiritual center and your capacity to be in the now.

This is a profound psychological shift and represents the capacity to accept the sense of emptiness or nothingness that exists at the center. This is what Heidegger referred to as the "ground of being," where there are no thoughts or feelings to anchor us but only the experience of the moment. It feels unfamiliar and strange and at times scary. But if you can stay with this sense of "emptiness" you will notice a profound sense of calm overtaking you and a sense of heightened awareness. You will feel your own feelings surge through your body and will begin to sense the enormous possibilities that exist for you in the world when you are living from the expanded vision of love that is reflected in forgiveness.

Rousseau wrote: "Take the course opposite to custom, you will almost always do well." Consciously avoid conforming to the social group at the expense of your uniqueness. Ignorance of the limitations set by others, coupled with time spent alone, nourishes imagination and achievement potential. If you take your lead from others, you will be frustrated and increasingly dependent on them and will limit your achievement. No doubt, you derive much satisfaction from your activities with others. But participation in groups should suit your interests and your time schedule and come from genuine desire, not a sense of obligation.

The search for happiness and a life free of problems will bring less satisfaction to you than involvement in productive activity. A permanent state of comfort is incompatible with existence. Efforts to achieve it are likely to fail. Maximum involvement in present activity dispels egotism, false pride, petty jealousy, and wasteful competitiveness and brings real satisfaction.

According to John Foster, one of the strongest characteristics of genius is the "power of lighting its own fire." Those who accomplish much have a unifying purpose to their life and express themselves in whatever manner, shape, or form is necessary to achieve their purpose. Call it simplicity, humility, or self-sufficiency. You may believe that a Stravinsky, an Einstein, or a Picasso has, by his genius, earned the right to be eccentric, idiosyncratic, self-willed. I contend that the decision to become masters of their own fate gave them the courage to try new things. The willingness to think the unthinkable requires courage to spend time alone, to run the risk of ridicule. Not everyone is a Picasso, but everyone can consciously distinguish himself from the world around him.

Set aside time to pursue your own objectives. This will give you the strength and capacity to express your uniqueness. Light your own fire. Pursue your own objectives without fear of failure, censure, or criticism. This will free that unique combination of factors that lie buried beneath your social-self. Many of your conflicts may very well be due to the suppression of this inner self. To the extent that you can discover your inner self, you will be able to bypass many of the numerous conflicting expectations that are imposed upon you by the complexities of modern society. The more you follow a fixed course, the more you will be able to become that which you are capable of becoming. You shouldn't have to modify or accommodate yourself to each new situation. It's easier to be yourself wherever you are. Where conformity governs you, you will be continually shifting from situation to situation.

Set limits in your personal relationships. At work, avoid those involvements that distract you from your job. Avoid ill-defined helping situations that engender feelings of exploitation. If concern about the responses of others hampers your self-expression, don't seek out leadership or managerial roles. Find situations in which you can comfortably assert yourself without worrying about negative feedback from others. You can change your mind more readily if you have said no instead of yes. If you have difficulty saying no and tend to overcommit yourself, don't make decisions hastily. Take time to think things through.

No one can get along without some assumptions about the nature of the world. In the broadest sense, a philosophy of life or a religion provides this perspective. It is a framework of expectations about life and rationalizations about misfortune that are handed down from parent to child in the form of spoken and unspoken traditions and prejudices. These expectations are only slowly modified as the individual tests his mettle against the realities of the world. In a sense, this is what anthropologists refer to as culture, the commonly shared perceptions, beliefs, and attitudes about the nature of the world.

CONCLUSION

EVERYONE FEELS INADEQUATE FROM TIME to time. Some even feel inadequate all of the time. Feelings of inadequacy are generated by a comparison of oneself to others, not failure to accomplish a task.

When you feel inadequate, stop for a minute and consider what you do have. Do you have your health? Do you have friends? Do you have free time? There will always be something positive in what you do have. Ultimately, satisfaction will come from those activities you pursue from the position you are in now.

Reaching an objective may not satisfy you for long. Therefore, you must seek new objectives to pursue. Satisfaction comes from the process of pursuing your vision, not the attainment of it. Of course, achievement will make you feel good. But the feeling won't last. Your mind needs new activity.

Your mental activity is as much a part of you as your heartbeat and respiratory rhythm. Your life is neither the activity outside yourself nor the organization you belong to, and you can't really define yourself accordingly.

You will find peace of mind when you determine and act in terms of your own nature and in terms of your vision. Greater understanding of the power your thoughts have in influencing your state of being and becoming will bring you much satisfaction. This understanding will result also in a greater appreciation of the differences between yourself and others, who have their own characteristic thoughts and attitudes. You will find satisfaction when you stop trying to affect the results of things directly and concentrate only on the causes that you can use to accomplish your dream.

A sense of humor can also provide perspective and the capacity to differentiate yourself from the situation in which you find yourself. You may also gain objectivity through prayer or physical activity. Develop one such technique to use when pessimism or a negative frame of mind occurs. Shift to it before you have made serious mistakes in handling a problem. Swift said, "Although men are accused of not knowing their own weakness, yet perhaps few know their own strength. It is men, as in soils, where sometimes there is a vein of gold which the owner knows not of." The time you are wasting thinking about your inadequacy could be spent searching for that vein of gold in your activities and yourself.

This book has been written on the premise that you can stop living on automatic pilot run by programmed patterns of the past. You can consciously choose a new way of being in the world, a framework for realizing your full human potential. This new perspective of the world will serve to stimulate a variety of hidden and untapped potentials that, until now, were dormant or suppressed.

Your vision will provide a guideline for making order out of chaos and give purpose and energy to your everyday actions. Focusing on something outside yourself provides a larger meaning, direction, purpose, and intensity to your life and enables you to be more present to your experience.

When you begin to live in the world through the perspective of a vision, you begin to see new connections and possibilities that call into play new behaviors and new opportunities for expressing yourself. You are able to access the future in a new way by listening to everything as an opportunity related to the vision and are able to find new ways for tapping into your capacity to be fully engaged in the moment before you.

DAILY CHECKLIST

1. Work to improve that which you do best and most readily. As much as possible, rely on yourself to accomplish the goals you have set for yourself.
2. Concentrate first on activities related to the objectives that are most important to you. Much can be accomplished in a short time if you devote yourself to your highest priorities. Keep track of time expended in activities so that you can better monitor your daily routines. Don't succumb to the feeling that you have insufficient time to do what you want. If you focus on your major objectives, you will minimize or halt those activities that have no real importance. You will be increasingly free

of the pressure to pursue less important activities.

3. Prepare a general schedule the night before, but approach each day in a relaxed way, letting things emerge and evolve as the day goes on. Above all, seek activities that you enjoy. When you finish one activity, move on to another.

4. Focused and informed activity reduces fear and anxiety. Study of a task and the actual effort of testing it lead to knowledge. Remembering this will take the sting out of failure, which, in fact, should be a source of new information that can assist you when you return to the task. Criticism, however unpleasant, can provide valuable information about ways to improve. Make the most of the information and resources you now have, and don't dwell on potential sources of difficulty that are beyond the limited amount of information available to you. This will only magnify illusions of fear and anxiety. Postponement can become habitual and can lead to nonproductivity.

Don't procrastinate by fantasizing about past failures or future problems; don't allow yourself to be distracted by opportunities for self-indulgence. When you postpone an activity, you increase the chances of never accomplishing it, and you will be left with memories of past wishes rather than of past deeds.

5. How you handle an anxiety-producing situation—on the job, in the home, or in the community—will depend on your own particular temperament, constitution, previous training, and experience. Don't resort to mechanical formulas to solve problems. Find the method most compatible with your own personality and life-style. You can learn from emulating others, but you should strive to conduct your life in ways suited to yourself. New situations require new solutions. The more you look for your own solutions to new and problematic situations, the more likely you will find the best approach for you. Don't blame your inaction on others and take credit for sacrificing

your vision on their behalf. This demeans them and creates insecurity about your "true feelings."

6. Acting in terms of your vision will give you strength in dealing with the most complex situations and will minimize the psychological threats of specific situations. Ultimately, what you accomplish results from your willingness to be true to yourself. Stick to what you find most rewarding. This will make your life more rewarding and will minimize your conflicts.

7. The strongest relationships develop from pursuit of a common objective or activity. This shared experience increases tolerance for differences in attitudes and values and reduces efforts to try to change others for the sake of the relationship. Relationships that focus simply on "having a relationship" can prove taxing and frustrating. Similarly, guard against a willingness to be so accommodating that you compromise your own identity.

8. The key to transformation is recognizing how trapped you are by the mind. Learn to notice

how you keep getting caught in mind traps and learn to let go of them by observing the processes and allowing yourself to really be. To surrender you must reframe the context of the experience. See how you are trapped by your thinking and create a new way of seeing the world. The solution is in transcending, not eliminating the trap or suppressing your responses.

9. Surrender means to get to a point where you can be free from the self-conscious processes and mental gymnastics that now govern your life. It is based on the assumption that you already have all the potential that you need to make your life work. It is OK to be who you are and to choose the potential, interest, and inclination that you already have. You don't have to keep searching for confirmation by focusing on being someone else or being somewhere else. Surrender yourself to the next moment. Accept your potential and the world of reality as it is, trusting that everything is as it was intended to be.

10. In effect, despite the way you have been brought up, life is not something to be gained. Rather it is a time or space in which to express what you already have and who you already are. When you choose what you have rather than try to escape from it, you reduce the internal split or separation that causes all the suffering. Only when you accept who you are and what you are trying to hide can you come alive in your life. Accept events as they are. Allow time for things to develop, and stop pushing for closure or certainty. Krishnamurti wrote about this in very clear language: "It is not that you must be free from fear. The moment you try to free yourself from fear, you create a resistance against fear. Resistance, in any form, does not end fear. What is needed, rather than running away or controlling or suppressing or any other resistance, is understanding fear; that means, watch it, learn about it, come directly into contact with it. We are to learn about fear, not how to escape from it, not how to resist it through courage and so on."

11. You already have all that you need. Your task is merely to choose what you have and to express your hidden potential by being willing to live with uncertainty and by digging deeper into yourself to find the way. The key here is taking action rather than remaining in your thoughts. What is it that you dreamed of doing as a child? What is it that you would choose for yourself if you could have anything or do anything that you wanted to have or do? What would be your major choice if you could temporarily put aside self-doubts, fears, and uncertainties? What action can you take that is consistent with your vision? What can you do in the next moment to move the action forward? Consider these questions and then focus on relaxing into actions that are consistent with your vision while letting go of the distracting concerns about results, wins, failures, obstacles, and problems. As Shunryu Suzuki wrote: "The result is not the point; it is the effort to improve ourselves that is valuable. There is no end to this practice."